ANCIENT MEDICINE

Andrew Langley

Raintree

Chicago, Illinois

www.capstonepub.com
Visit our website to find out more information about Heinemann-Raintree books.

To order:
☎ Phone 800-747-4992
🖳 Visit www.capstonepub.com
to browse our catalog and order online.

Edited by Andrew Farrow, Adam Miller, and
 Vaarunika Dharmapala
Designed by Philippa Jenkins
Original illustrations © Capstone Global Library
 Ltd 2013
Illustrations by Oxford Designers & Illustrators
Picture research by Ruth Blair
Originated by Capstone Global Library Ltd
Printed and bound in China by Leo Paper
 Products Ltd

16 15 14 13 12
10 9 8 7 6 5 4 3 2 1

Library of Congress Cataloging-in-Publication Data
Langley, Andrew.
 Ancient medicine / Andrew Langley.
  p. cm. — (Medicine through the ages)
 Includes bibliographical references and index.
 ISBN 978-1-4109-4642-3 (hb : freestyle) — ISBN 978-1-4109-4648-5 (pb : freestyle) 1. Medicine, Ancient. 2. Medicine — History. I. Title.
 R135.L36 2013
 910.9′01 — dc23 2011031886

Acknowledgments
We would like to thank the following for permission to reproduce photographs: Alamy pp. 17 (© Hemis), 18 (© Prisma Bildagentur AG); Getty Images pp. 6 (Jane Sweeney/Robert Harding), 7 (SSPL), 9, 10, 13 (The Bridgeman Art Library), 20 (AFP), 28 (Hulton Archive), 29 (DEA/G. Dagli Orti), 39 (Danita Delimont/Gallo Images); Photolibrary pp. 15 (Still Pictures), 24 (Norbert Reismann/Doc-Stock), 27 (Leonardo Diaz Romero/Age Fotostock), 30 (Robert Harding Travel), 38 (Photoservice Electa), 40 (Imagebroker RF/Guenter Fischer); Science Photo Library pp. 16 (Mark De Fraeye), 34 (Sheila Terry); Shutterstock pp. 5 (© Stuart Elflett), 8 (© Efremova Irina); Topfoto p. 12 (Charles Walker); Wellcome Library pp.14, 19 (Mark de Fraeye); Wellcome Library, London pp. 11, 21, 22, 23, 25, 26, 31, 32, 33, 35, 36, 37.

Cover photograph of a Pompeiian fresco showing the battle wounds of Aeneas, from the Archaeological Museum of Naples, Italy, reproduced with permission of Science Photo Library (Sheila Terry).

Disclaimer
All the Internet addresses (URLs) given in this book were valid at the time of going to press. However, due to the dynamic nature of the Internet, some addresses may have changed, or sites may have changed or ceased to exist since publication. While the author and publisher regret any inconvenience this may cause readers, no responsibility for any such changes can be accepted by either the author or the publisher.

Contents

Some words are shown in bold, **like this**. You can find out what they mean by looking in the glossary. You can also look out for them in the "Word Station" box at the bottom of each page.

The Beginnings of Medicine

The practices and theories we use to **diagnose**, cure, and prevent disease are known as medicine. Nobody knows for certain when it began, but it is probably as old as we are. It is likely that there has been illness ever since human society started about 2 million years ago. In their search for food and shelter, early humans would have been injured, caught infections, or suffered from other diseases. So, very soon, they started to develop ways to treat these problems.

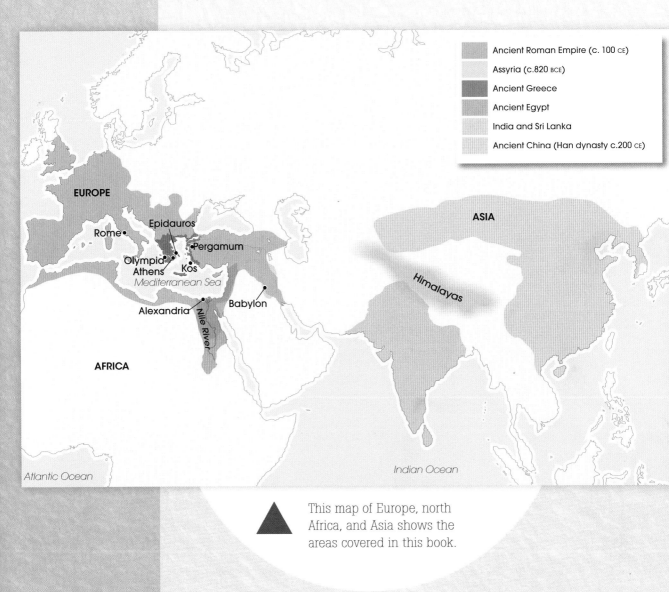

Ancient Roman Empire (c. 100 CE)
Assyria (c.820 BCE)
Ancient Greece
Ancient Egypt
India and Sri Lanka
Ancient China (Han dynasty c.200 CE)

EUROPE

Rome
Epidauros
Pergamum
Olympia
Athens
Kos
Mediterranean Sea
Alexandria
Nile River
Babylon

AFRICA

ASIA

Himalayas

Atlantic Ocean

Indian Ocean

This map of Europe, north Africa, and Asia shows the areas covered in this book.

WORD STATION
diagnose identify the nature of a disease or injury through examination

Insects such as flies and mosquitoes carried disease throughout human settlements.

Hunters and gatherers

Most early humans were hunter-gatherers, who moved around looking for plants and catching animals to eat. These people lived active lives. On average, men lived until they were 35 years old. Women had shorter lives, partly because of the dangers of pregnancy and childbirth.

Still, these first humans do not seem to have suffered from many deadly diseases. This may be because they lived in small groups and did not stay in one place for long. There was little opportunity for infections to pass from one person to another. The main causes of death were warfare, harsh climates, and poor food.

The rise of disease

By about 8000 BCE, things began to change. Many people stopped their nomadic (wandering) way of life and lived in permanent settlements. They cleared the forests to make farmland. They grew plants as food crops and kept animals to provide meat and milk.

The new lifestyle exposed them to more infections. Cattle and other herd animals carried their own diseases. Settlements attracted rats. They were also often near water sources, which were ideal breeding grounds for disease-carrying insects. Finally, because they stayed in one place, people were at greater risk of being infected by the same disease time after time.

COMMON CONFUSIONS

What is prehistoric?

Some people think the word *prehistoric* refers to cavemen. This is wrong. The word *prehistory* means "before history." This refers to the age after life began on Earth, but before writing was invented. Without writing, early humans were unable to make records of what they did.

There is no definite date when prehistory ended. Human societies in different parts of the world developed at different rates, and some invented writing much earlier than others.

Medicine and magic

Prehistoric people did not know what caused deadly diseases. If the sickness had no obvious cause, they believed it was sent by the gods. It might be a sign that the gods were angry because the people had done something wicked. Sickness might also be caused by something else—an evil spirit, or someone who had cursed the diseased person.

These causes were supernatural, which means "outside nature." So they were usually treated by a **shaman**. Each tribal group had a shaman, who was a combination of a priest and a doctor. The shaman was believed to have special contact with the gods. He could draw on their power to cure a patient. This method would be used to drive evil spirits out of a sick person's body.

This modern-day shaman lives in a Zulu village in South Africa.

MAGICAL MEDICINE TODAY

There are shamans in several societies today, including in parts of Africa, South Korea, and Japan. They communicate with the spirit world and perform rituals to cure sickness. However, we do not know if they are similar to the "medicine men" of prehistoric times.

WORD STATION
shaman medicine man or priest who is believed to communicate with the spirit world

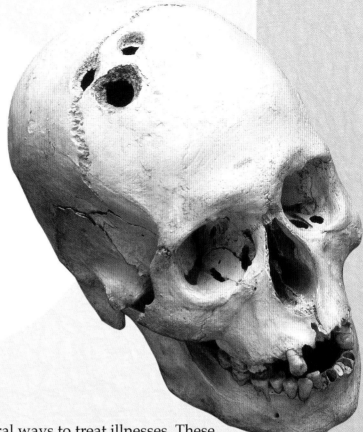

This human skull dates from 2200 to 2000 BCE. You can see that it has been trepanned, probably to release evil spirits. Three holes are visible. One of them is very big.

Herbs and holes in the head

People also figured out more natural ways to treat illnesses. These were mostly very simple, but they were the first examples of the scientific approach to medicine that humans have developed ever since.

If someone broke a bone, the injury might be protected by coating it in mud from the river and drying it in the sun. People used local plants as the first drugs, to soothe pain or help cuts to heal. The first form of **surgery** was called trepanning. This involved cutting a hole in the patient's skull, and it may have relieved headaches.

How do we know about prehistoric people?

There are no written records of early humans and their medical ideas. We can only find out about prehistoric medicine by looking at objects from that time. These include skeletons and other remains of bodies. By studying their bones, scientists can see how ancient people might have been affected by disease or injury.

Archaeologists can also learn about early humans by examining ancient tools, weapons, and other products. Cave paintings and other works of art give us clues about prehistoric beliefs and customs.

Egypt and the Middle East

By about 3000 BCE, many humans had settled down to become farmers. In these settlements, the world's first civilizations began. One of the greatest was ancient Egypt, in northeast Africa. Here, the Nile River created a long valley of lush land where crops grew easily. Egypt became wealthy and powerful, and its rulers built cities and huge monuments.

Crops grew well in the lush land of the Nile Valley. Disease lurked there, too, as well as in the surrounding desert.

Surviving the epidemics

Civilization also helped to cause the first **epidemics** of disease. As towns grew, more people lived close to each other, and to domestic animals. Merchants, soldiers, and other travelers carried infections from one place to another. Diseases such as **smallpox** spread quickly through crowded settlements, killing huge numbers of people.

WORD STATION
epidemic rapid spread of a disease through an area or population

The Egyptians and other people of the Middle East had no effective medicines or treatments for fighting these deadly diseases. Some could live through an epidemic because their bodies were naturally immune (resistant) to the infection. Later, however, they might be killed by another kind of disease.

Desert and river dangers

The ancient Egyptians suffered from many kinds of illnesses. Some sprang from the land of Egypt itself. People breathed in fine sand from the nearby desert areas, which lodged in their lungs and caused disease. Others were attacked by bilharzia worms, which lived in the mud of the Nile River. The worms burrowed into a person's body and damaged the **liver** and other **organs**.

How do we know about the diseases of people who lived over 3,000 years ago? Scientists have pushed special cameras called **endoscopes** into the lungs of mummified bodies and found traces of sand. Evidence for bilharzia damage can be seen in pictures from an ancient Egyptian tomb. This shows men with swollen body parts.

This ancient Egyptian painting shows preparations for a funeral. In the middle, you can see a sarcophagus, a highly decorated stone coffin.

MUMMIES AND MEDICINE

The ancient Egyptians believed a person's body should be preserved after death. They developed a way to dry out (mummify) the corpse so it would not decay. They removed the heart and other internal organs, then they dried the flesh with salts and wrapped it in cloth.

The first doctors

The civilization of ancient Egypt lasted for over 2,000 years. During that time, the Egyptians made many medical discoveries. Doctors specialized in different branches of medicine, including childbirth and animal bites. Each branch had its own god or goddess.

The most famous Egyptian doctor was treated as a god after his death. Imhotep, who lived around 2700 BCE, was a priest, a court official, and an architect. He was best known for his pioneering medical work. He **diagnosed** and treated many diseases and performed **surgery**.

Sorcerers and surgeons

Egyptians believed that most illnesses were caused by evil spirits. These entered a person through the mouth and other body openings. So the earliest doctors were also priests or sorcerers. They recited spells, gave the patient amulets (charms) to wear, or used lotions. These were meant to ward off the evil spirits.

Doctors saw that some treatments worked better than others. **Physicians** used **minerals** and plant and animal extracts to cure many diseases.

This statue of Imhotep dates from around 2980 BCE. In addition to his medical accomplishments, Imhotep is thought to have helped design the famous Step Pyramid at Saqqara.

WORD STATION
physician person qualified to practice medicine

One remedy for eye infections was made of onions, copper, acid, and sawdust. Other medicines included hippopotamus fat, black lizards, **opium**, and garlic.

Surgeons developed ways to treat external injuries. They cleaned wounds with special ointments or scorched them to stop bleeding. Then they bound them with linen bandages. More serious cuts were stitched, using copper needles. To set broken limbs, surgeons made casts with a mixture of cow's milk and barley.

Precious papyrus

Several sources tell us about Egyptian medicine. These are medical "textbooks" written on rolls of papyrus (a kind of paper made from reeds). The two most important are named after the historians who discovered them:

- The Edwin Smith papyrus: Written in about 1600 BCE, it lists details of over 40 different injuries and how to treat them.

- The Ebers papyrus: Dating from about 1550 BCE, this describes over 700 recipes for medicines and cures.

COMMON CONFUSIONS

Did the Egyptians cut up corpses?

Ancient Egyptian **embalmers** prepared corpses for mummification by removing organs from inside the body (see page 9). However, this did not mean they **dissected** corpses to study them. In fact, many historians think dissection was forbidden in ancient Egypt.

The Edwin Smith (left) and Ebers documents were not written in the ancient Egyptian picture writing called hieroglyphs, but rather in a related form called hieratic script.

The tablets of the Two Rivers

Egypt was not the only ancient civilization in the region. From about 3500 BCE, there had been several great kingdoms in Mesopotamia. This was the fertile "land between the rivers" — the Tigris and the Euphrates — and is now part of modern-day Iraq. The people who lived there also made early advances in medicine.

We know this because of records found by archaeologists, including a pillar from the kingdom of Babylon. In about 1780 BCE, the Babylonian King Hammurabi had the Code of Laws carved on this pillar. They include rules for doctors, such as how much they should be paid. They also say that if a wealthy person called a lord died during surgery, the doctor's hand would be chopped off!

Other records come from the Assyrian kingdom in about 660 BCE. They were scratched on clay writing tablets that were stored in the library of King Assurbanipal. Many give details of how to diagnose illnesses, along with ways to cure them. Some of these sound similar to modern problems, such as tuberculosis (an infection of the lungs) and jaundice (liver disease).

This carving on top of the pillar of Hammurabi shows the king of Babylon (left) being given the Code of Laws by a god.

Hebrew healers

The Hebrews founded a civilization in what is now Israel in about 1020 BCE. Similar to other ancient peoples, they believed that disease was sent from God as punishment for wrongdoing. However, the Hebrews also developed practical ways to prevent and treat diseases.

Their main weapon was **hygiene**. By keeping clothes, bodies, and dwellings clean, they lessened the chance of infection.

Quarantine

The Hebrews invented the process of quarantine, in which patients are kept isolated from other people so they cannot pass on their illness.

The word *quarantine* comes from the Italian word *quarantena*, which means a period of 40 days. This was the length of time people had to be isolated before doctors could be certain whether or not they had a disease. However, the ancient Hebrews used a much shorter period. The book of Leviticus, in the Jewish Bible, says that people suspected of having leprosy (an infectious disease) should be isolated for seven days.

After this, they were examined by a priest. If the infection had gone, they were released. If the infection was still the same, they were kept for another seven days.

This sculpture shows a god holding a nail. It was a foundation nail, which the ancient Mesopotamians fixed to temple walls to show that a god lived there.

THE FIRST WOMEN DOCTORS

One of the earliest known female doctors was Peseshet. Her name appears on a monument in an Egyptian tomb near Giza. She is described as "head of lady physicians" and probably lived in about 2500 BCE. Some women also worked as doctors and **midwives** in ancient Mesopotamia.

India

In about 1500 BCE, Aryan people from central Asia began settling in India. By 500 BCE, they had built up a strong and wealthy civilization in the north. These early Indians developed their own language, called Sanskrit, and their own religion, called Hinduism. They also created their own kind of medicine.

Ayurvedic medicine

Like most other ancient peoples, the Indians closely connected their medical ideas with their religious faith. The main system of healing was called *Ayurveda*, a Sanskrit word meaning "the knowledge needed for a long life." It was based on the Vedas, the sacred books of the early Indian religion that became Hinduism.

Dhanvantari is important in the Hindu tradition. He is physician to the gods and the god of Ayurvedic medicine. In his four arms he holds a conch, a disc, leeches for **bloodletting**, and the nectar of immortality (living forever). This statue stands outside a hospital in Mumbai, India.

Keeping clean by bathing in the water of sacred rivers, such as the Ganges, is an important part of Hindu life.

Ayurvedic medicine was part of a practical guide to living. It recommended ways to stay healthy and to prevent sickness, as well as cures. Doctors stressed the importance of **hygiene**, a good diet, and regular exercise, which were linked to the rituals of the Hindu faith.

Ayurvedic **physicians** believed that bodies contained certain amounts of important substances. These included blood, wind, **bile** (stomach acid), and phlegm (mucus). Illness was caused when the balance between these substances was disturbed.

Doctors also specified 107 important points on the human body, called *marmas*. These were usually at places where important features, such as **arteries**, nerves, and tendons, were near the surface of the skin. An injury at any of these points could be deadly, though they could also be massaged to promote healing.

Training to be a doctor

A person training to be a doctor was expected to behave like a priest. As a student, he was forbidden to eat meat, have sex, or carry weapons. He had to be truthful, honest, and obedient to his master. He could only examine or treat women if their husband or guardian were present. All doctors had to take a professional vow, similar to the **Hippocratic Oath** in the West (see page 30).

COMMON CONFUSIONS

Ayurvedic medicine today

Ayurvedic medicine is still practiced across India, Asia, Europe, and the United States. However, it is not the same as the ancient Ayurveda, which used only plant extracts to make potions and cures. Today, most doctors in India prescribe antibiotics and other Western drugs.

WORD STATION
Hippocratic Oath oath taken by a doctor, promising to observe a code of medical behavior based on the teachings of Hippocrates

15

How do we know about ancient Indian medicine?

Ayurvedic medicine was founded on the four sacred books called the Vedas. Two other very early Sanskrit texts, which describe the practical side of medicine in ancient India, have survived the centuries. Nobody knows exactly when they were written, but experts believe they are about 2,000 years old.

The first was called the *Caraka Samhita*, or "Caraka's Collection." It deals mainly with the care a doctor must take in observing and **diagnosing** over 200 kinds of sickness. The second text is the *Susruta Samhita*, or "Susruta's Collection." This contains a large section on **surgery**. Both texts give recipes for many medicines, using a huge variety of materials including snake dung, camel urine, honey, flowers, and gold.

Pioneers of surgery

The ancient Indians were the first people to make major advances in surgery. Susruta describes how a huge variety of operations were performed. Indian surgeons could remove **kidney stones** and drain fluid from wounds. They had over 120 different instruments for these tasks.

Many Ayurvedic medicines are still prepared the same way they were prepared in ancient times. Here, herbs are being heated to extract their essence.

WORD STATION
kidney stone hard object made of crystallized salts that forms in the kidney

Herbs and spices are crushed and pounded together in a stone pestle.

Susruta also made experiments in plastic surgery. His text explains how flaps of skin from one part of the body can be moved to cover a defect in another part. To cover a nose injury, for example, a surgeon would cut a piece of skin from the patient's forehead (a close match of nose skin). This was sewn in place over the nose. Plastic surgeons use very similar techniques today.

The ashtangas

Ayurvedic doctors divided medicine into *ashtangas* (from the Sanskrit language, meaning "eight parts"):

- internal medicine (inside the body)
- childbirth and diseases of children
- surgery
- treatment of the head region (eyes, ears, nose, and throat)
- preventing infectious diseases
- possession by evil spirits (probably an early kind of **psychiatry**)
- the curing of poisons and detoxifying (cleansing) the body
- love potions (to help couples have children).

Treating problems of the mind

The Indians were pioneers in the study and treatment of psychiatric problems. They thought that the mind, like the body, contained certain important elements. Mental disease was caused when the balance of these elements was disturbed. The aim of treatment was to restore this mental balance.

Some doctors believed the disturbance was the work of invisible spirits, including devils and ghosts of the dead (called *bhoota*). Others thought it was caused by **microbes** in the air that were too tiny to see. The main treatment used the burning of special herbs to make the air free of these germs.

Diseases in children

An entire branch of Ayurvedic medicine was devoted to treating diseases of children. Here again, evil spirits were blamed for causing many illnesses. Fevers, vomiting (throwing up), and other stomach disorders, for example, were seen as attacks by demons called *grahas* (Sanskrit for "child-seizers"). Doctors treated these problems with chants and herbs. The chants, or "mantras," were sacred words or phrases repeated many times over the patient. The herbs were burned to cleanse the air.

Ayurvedic doctors used chants, called mantras, to help healing. Mantras were sometimes carved on stones to help prayer and meditation.

WORD STATION
microbe tiny organism (living thing) that can carry disease

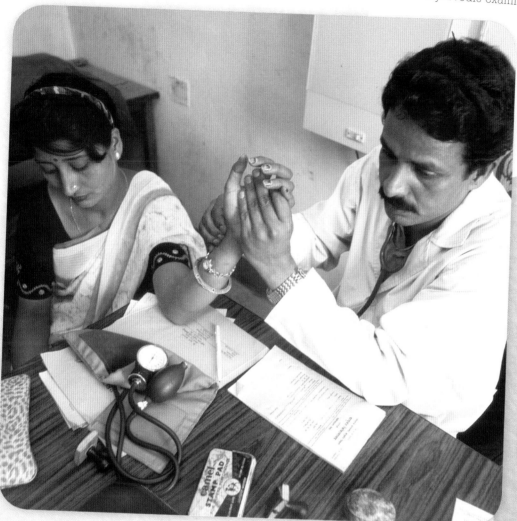

Taking a patient's pulse is an important part of an Ayurvedic examination.

Channels of the body

One of the most important aspects of Ayurvedic medicine dealt with the *srotas* (Sanskrit for "inner channels"). These channels carry important chemicals around the body. The different *srotas* transport food, water, blood, air, bone marrow, fat, and many other substances to areas where they are needed.

Ayurvedic doctors believed that disease occurs when these channels got damaged or blocked. They had several ways of opening them up again. Among these were massage and steam baths, which caused the patient to sweat.

China

China began as a collection of independent states. It was unified for the first time in 221 BCE, and it was ruled by an emperor and a strong central government. During this period, the country developed rapidly. The arts, science, and education all flourished. Systems for writing and measuring were invented, and a large part of the Great Wall was built.

Early discoveries

Chinese medicine also developed quickly. It became a respected profession, separate from religion and **sorcery**. The early Chinese made many important discoveries about how the human body works and how disease and injury can be treated. Doctors were trained in a state system. There were two types of doctors—those who cared for the emperor and his court, and those who cared for the army and ordinary people.

Many elements of ancient Chinese medicine are still used in China today. These people are having herbs applied to special points on their bodies.

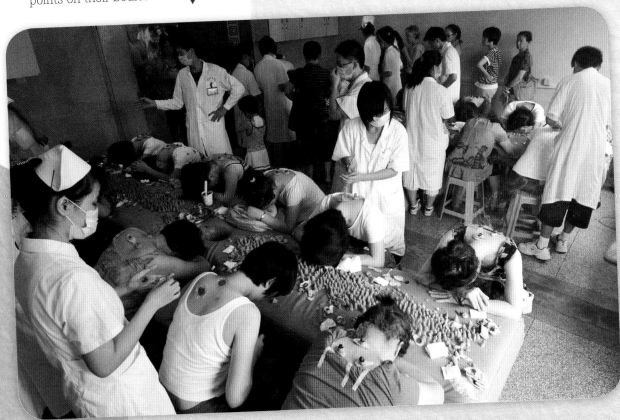

WORD STATION
sorcery taking action by communicating with the world of spirits, as in witchcraft

This illustration is from a Chinese book published in 1439. It shows a master instructing students in medical knowledge.

The body in harmony

The ancient Chinese based their ideas about sickness and health on a belief in harmony. They thought that all the parts of the human body had to be kept in harmony, or they would not work properly. This would make the person become sick.

The Chinese believed that the body — like nature — was made up of five basic elements. These were fire, water, earth, wood, and metal. Doctors aimed to cure disease by restoring the balance of these elements inside the patient.

The Chinese also believed that the world was ruled by a pair of forces called *yin* and *yang*. *Yin* means "the shady side of the hill," and *yang* means "the sunny side of the hill." These two forces were opposites, but they could only exist together.

Chinese doctors thought there was a constant struggle in the body between the forces of *yin* and *yang*. For instance, if a person was very angry, then *yang* was gaining control. The doctor's job was to treat the patient and return *yin* and *yang* to their proper balance.

COMMON CONFUSIONS

Have there been any advances in Chinese medicine?

Traditional medicine in China has hardly changed since ancient times. Doctors have great respect for tradition and have followed teachings and texts that are over 2,000 years old. It was only in the 20th century that some Western methods were adopted in China.

Diagnosis and treatment

Chinese doctors were trained to examine their patients very carefully. First, they looked at a patient's appearance. What color were the face and eyes? Did the patient feel hot? Was he or she breathing normally? Was the patient's digestion working properly? Then, they asked a patient's family members for details of the patient's medical history.

The next step was to take the patient's pulse. The pulse was measured at several different parts of each wrist. This gave the doctor a detailed picture of how the energy forces (called *chi*) were flowing through the body, and it showed where there might be an imbalance between *yin* and *yang*.

The most important form of medical treatment was with drugs. Chinese **physicians** had a huge range to choose from — more than 16,000 different prescriptions, using over 2,000 ingredients. Many of these were intended to control the flow of *chi* or to heat up or cool parts of the body. As with today's medicines, these drugs were taken as pills, powders, or liquids.

Chinese doctors measured the pulse at various points on the patient's body, including the wrist.

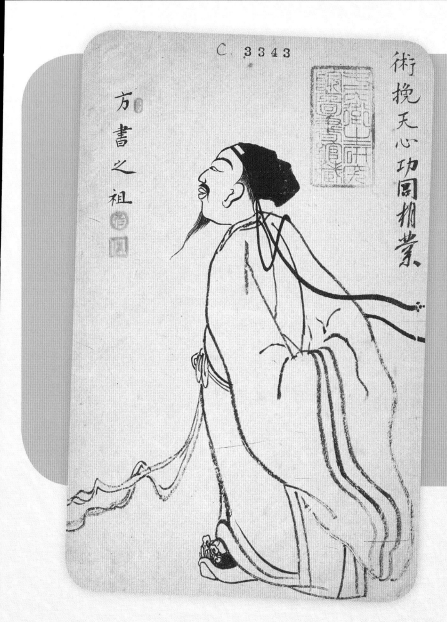

方書之祖

術挽天心功固相業

ZHANG ZHONGJING
Chinese physician
(c. 150 CE – 219 CE)

Zhang Zhongjing was born in Henan province in China. We know very little about his life, but several of his medical texts have survived. The most famous of these is called *On Cold Damage*. It explains ways of treating some of the infectious diseases that were raging in China at the time.

The Yellow Emperor's Book

The earliest writings about Chinese medicine are in a manual from about 200 BCE. This was written as a conversation between a legendary Chinese emperor (known as "the Yellow Emperor") and his ministers and is known as *The Yellow Emperor's Book*. It was the basis of all Chinese medical thought, and it is still admired today.

The text is in two main parts. In the first, the Yellow Emperor discusses how to live and be healthy in a natural way, as well as the meaning of the life forces of *yin* and *yang*. In the second part, he examines **acupuncture** and how it can be used to treat sickness. (For more on acupuncture, see pages 24–25.)

Getting the needle

Acupuncture has been widely used for over 2,000 years. This unusual treatment was first described in *The Yellow Emperor's Book*. Thin needles were pushed into the skin to different depths. Then they are turned or vibrated. These needles were originally made of bone or stone, but later they were made of metal.

The Chinese believed that the energy force called *chi* flowed through a person along special channels. The aim of acupuncture was to control this flow. By inserting needles at carefully chosen points on the body, the doctor could affect the balance of energy. One of the most popular uses of acupuncture was to relieve pain.

Another way to control the flow of *chi* was by burning tiny pellets at the same chosen points on the body. The pellets were made of a herb called moxa, which was dried and powdered. The treatment was known as moxibustion (the burning of moxa). Doctors thought the heat from the burning warmed the energy channels and made them work better.

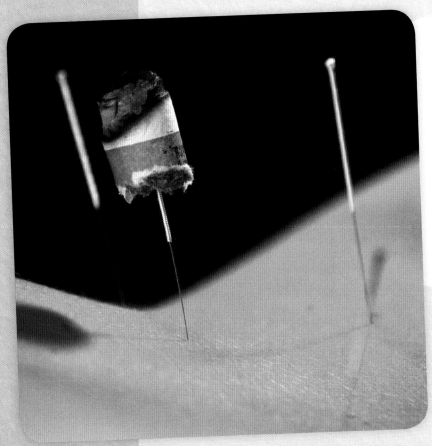

Here you can see moxibustion in action. The herb moxa is burning on the end of a needle. The needle has been placed at a special point on the body.

WORD STATION
anatomy bodily structure of a human, animal, or plant

What have we learned from Chinese medicine?

The ancient Chinese, like the Egyptians, were forbidden from cutting up and examining dead bodies. Therefore, they knew very little about human **anatomy**. Few of their ideas about the balance of elements and forces in the body have become part of modern medicine.

However, some treatments, such as acupuncture, are still used today. Chinese physicians also made several important discoveries about medicine. Here are some of them:

- The Chinese knew that blood was pumped through the body by the heart. This was not known in Europe until about 1550 CE.

- Chinese doctors believed human bodies behaved differently depending on the time of the day or the months. This was confirmed by U.S. scientists in the 20th century, who discovered that asthma sufferers, for example, often get their worst attacks at night.

- If our food lacks certain **nutrients** called vitamins, we will suffer from certain diseases. The Chinese knew this over 1,700 years ago.

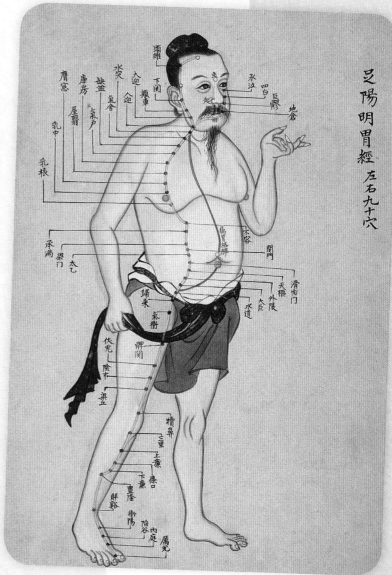

 This chart shows the acupuncture points on the body.

WORD STATION
nutrient substance that feeds or nourishes something

Greece

Greek civilization developed from about 800 BCE. At first, there was no central ruler. People lived in separate city-states, of which the most powerful were Athens, Corinth, Sparta, and Thebes. Even so, the Greeks saw themselves as held together by a common culture, and they founded the world's first democratic systems of government. Greek culture spread widely around the Mediterranean Sea.

This modern engraving shows a patient making a sacrifice at the ancient Greek temple of Epidauros (see page 27). His leg is being licked by a sacred snake.

Illness and the gods

The Greeks had their own stories about gods and goddesses and how the world was created. These stories are called myths. One myth explained how illness began. The goddess Pandora opened a forbidden jar or box and released all kinds of evil into the world—including diseases.

The Greeks believed that sickness and injury were caused by the gods. This is shown clearly in plays and poetry such as Homer's epic poem *The Iliad* (written in about 750 BCE). It opens with the god Apollo sending a plague to infect the Greek army, as a way to punish the Greek leader for disobedience.

Temple treatments

If the gods could cause diseases, surely they could cure them as well? People linked certain gods with healing powers and visited their shrines to look for help. The best-known Greek god of healing was Asklepios, who became very popular in about 500 BCE.

Temples were built all over the Greek world for the worship of Asklepios. The biggest was at Epidauros, in southern Greece. Thousands of people went there every year to pray for cures for disease. Many slept there, hoping that Asklepios would appear to them in dreams. He would heal them or give them advice on how to treat their illness.

Statues of Asklepios, such as this one, were always shown with the symbols of a rod and a snake.

The early Greeks and health

Male beauty and fitness were important to the ancient Greeks. Warriors and athletes were respected and admired, and the first Olympic Games were held in Greece in 776 BCE. Men spent a lot of time training in sports and other activities to keep themselves fit and healthy. Women did not take part in these activities, as they were discouraged from appearing in public.

Many early Greek doctors specialized in physical training and fitness. Others dealt with the injuries suffered by soldiers in local wars. Wounds were cleaned with wine or vinegar (which were known to kill harmful germs) and dressed with herbs. Then they were bound up tight to stop the bleeding.

These men appear on a Greek vase from the 400s BCE. The scene shows athletes training for the Olympic Games, watched by their trainer.

This marble carving shows a Greek **physician** treating a patient.

Natural causes of disease

Gradually, Greek philosophers explored the idea that diseases were not all the work of the gods, but rather had natural causes. Like other ancient peoples, they believed that the body contained a number of important fluids. For a person to be healthy, these had to be kept in balance.

In about 470 BCE, the philosopher Alcmaeon argued that humans experienced feelings through the brain, rather than the heart. In about 460 BCE, the thinker Democritus became the first person to suggest that everything was made up of tiny particles, which he called atoms. He also stated that babies were created by the mixing of "seeds" from both parents. We now know that all these ideas were correct.

At about the same time, Empedocles described the four elements of nature: earth, air, fire, and water. These were reflected in what Greeks called the four "**humors,**" which they believed were contained inside the human body. These humors, with their different qualities, were thought to control a person's health and temperament.

THE GREAT PLAGUE OF ATHENS

In 430 BCE, and again three years later, the people of Athens were struck by a deadly infectious disease. It caused vomiting, bleeding, and blindness. The infection spread quickly, and many thousands of people died. The disease caused panic, not just because it was deadly, but also because doctors did not know what caused it or how to treat it. People tried praying to the gods for help, but in vain. Even today, historians are not sure what kind of disease this was.

The mystery of Hippocrates

The most famous of all ancient Greek doctors was Hippocrates. His work was celebrated because it helped to separate medicine from religion, and also to establish it as a profession. Doctors around the world today still take the **Hippocratic Oath** (see the box below).

Very little is known about Hippocrates' life or his actual work. Historians think he was born on the Aegean island of Kos about 460 BCE. Here, he may have been taught medical skills by his father and started a school of medicine. Later, he possibly worked as a physician in Greece.

The Hippocratic Oath

For over 2,000 years, the Hippocratic Oath has been recited by medical students when they become doctors.

Among the promises they make are:

- to use their power to help the sick, and never to do harm
- never to give a patient a fatal poison, even if asked
- not to cut open the body (which is the work of surgeons)
- never to engage in sexual contact with patients
- to keep secret anything they are told by a patient.

This mosaic floor shows Hippocrates welcoming Asklepios to his medical center on the island of Kos.

Hippocrates advised doctors to examine a patient thoroughly. This plaster carving shows the god Asklepios on the right.

The Hippocratic writings

The main source of knowledge about Hippocratic medicine is in a collection of texts known as the Hippocratic writings. Nobody knows for sure whether Hippocrates actually wrote any of them. They were probably written by several people over a long period, then collected together.

These writings give us a detailed picture of the great advances made by Greek medicine around 400 BCE. There are case histories of patients, studies of **epidemics**, thoughts on the theory of medicine, and notes on dealing with specific problems such as fractures and **epilepsy**.

The most important development was in **diagnosing** illness. Doctors were advised to observe a patient's **symptoms** very carefully. One of the texts says, "Nothing is random: overlook nothing." Eyes, skin, and temperature should all be studied, as well as anything that came out of the body, including breath, ear wax, and urine. The doctor should also listen closely to any noises inside the body (such as occurs with congested lungs).

The work of Aristotle

Greek philosophers pushed forward new ideas about medicine long after the age of Hippocrates. The greatest of these thinkers was Aristotle (384 to 322 BCE). He set out to investigate all of the natural world, including how the human body and mind worked.

Aristotle did practical research. He watched **embryos** developing in hens' eggs and decided that the heart was the center of all life and movement. From this, he argued that blood absorbed food from the intestines.

Aristotle also **dissected** the bodies of animals to examine the positions of the **organs** and vessels inside. His observations of living things were often astonishing. Certain insect features that he saw and wrote about were not noticed by anyone again until the microscope was invented in the 17th century.

Aristotle was the son of a doctor. He studied many disciplines, including biology, botany, chemistry, history, logic, philosophy, physics, political theory, psychology, and zoology.

WORD STATION
embryo animal in the very early stages of its development from a fertilized egg

This medieval woodcut shows the ancient Greek medical pioneers Herophilus and Erasistratus (right).

Medicine in Alexandria

Aristotle later became tutor to a prince, Alexander of Macedon. As Alexander the Great, the young man went on to conquer a huge empire. In 331 BCE, he founded the Egyptian city of Alexandria. With its museum and library, this became the most important medical center of the period, where a series of important discoveries about **anatomy** were made.

In about 300 BCE, Herophilus became the first scientist to identify important parts of the body systems that deal with digestion and reproduction (having young), including the **prostate** and the **duodenum**. He also showed that the nerve system was linked to the brain. At about the same time, Erasistratus was studying the heart. By dissecting it, he found that it contained four one-way valves. This proved that the heart worked as a pump, moving blood through the veins to the rest of the body.

These discoveries were possible because the rulers of Alexandria allowed the dissection of human bodies. This had always been forbidden by the Greeks. However, after about 250 BCE, nearly all dissections stopped. Nobody knows why this happened. Dissection would not be widely used again until the European Renaissance, over 1,500 years later.

COMMON CONFUSIONS

Did early Christians help the progress of science?

The library of Alexandria housed over 700,000 books, containing knowledge from all over the ancient world. In about 400 CE, it is thought to have been destroyed by Christian rioters, who burned the books. They believed it was a pagan (non-Christian) temple. Soon after, Christians also murdered Hypatia, the first great female mathematician in Alexandria.

WORD STATION
duodenum part of the small intestine that plays an important part in digesting food

Rome

As the Greek Empire grew weaker, Rome became the greatest power in the Mediterranean. By about 100 BCE, Romans had conquered all of Italy, as well as Spain, Greece, and parts of north Africa. Their empire expanded to include Britain, Germany, and parts of the Middle East. The Romans were strong and efficient rulers. They built roads and towns, established a legal code, and respected local cultures.

Early Roman medicine

At first, the Romans had few doctors. They believed people were responsible for keeping themselves healthy. Anyone who got sick should be treated by his or her own family. Doctors cost money, and they were often mocked as ignorant butchers.

This Roman painting shows a soldier wounded in battle. A doctor is trying to remove an arrowhead from the soldier's thigh, using a medical instrument.

WORD STATION
epilepsy disorder of the brain that can cause sudden attacks of convulsive movement

Greek thinkers had a great influence on Roman medicine. This medieval picture shows Plato, Anaxagoras, and Democritus.

COMMON CONFUSIONS

Did the Greeks invent atomic theory?

The first person to state that everything was made up of tiny particles was the Greek Democritus (see page 29). He called them atoms, from the Greek word *atomos*, meaning "something that cannot be divided." The Greek surgeon Asclepiades had the same idea. However, they did not know how tiny an atom really is, or how it works.

Modern scientists have shown that an atom is itself made of several kinds of particles combined together. They have also shown that an atom can be divided, by the process known as nuclear fission. This is what creates the energy for nuclear weapons and power stations.

The early Romans also used treatments based on religion and magic. Some believed that hot blood from a gladiator's throat could cure **epilepsy**. A head cold would disappear if the sufferer kissed a mule on the nose. Special chants were repeated to heal a **dislocated** joint.

The Greeks in Rome

But the Romans gained most of their medical knowledge from Greece and Egypt. The first doctor mentioned in written sources was a Greek surgeon who arrived in Rome in 219 BCE. Another, named Asclepiades (after the god of healing), came to Italy about 100 BCE.

Asclepiades ignored the traditional Greek theories of the four **humors**. He believed that the health of the body depended on the correct arrangement of the "atoms" and fluids inside. If these were blocked, the person became sick. Asclepiades treated this with gentle exercise, bathing, and massage. He also recommended drinking wine.

Galen

The biggest medical celebrity in ancient Rome was Galen of Pergamum. He was a Greek who lived from 129 to 216 CE. He worked in Rome for much of his life, treating mainly wealthy and powerful people, including the Roman emperor Marcus Aurelius.

Galen was a showman. He first became famous in Rome by giving public displays in which he cut up various animals, some of them still alive. These included pigs, dogs, goats, and an elephant's heart. He once removed the intestines of an ape and then replaced them. He even used to ask his audience to decide which parts he should **dissect**.

We know a lot about Galen, mainly because he wrote a huge amount about himself and his work. He is thought to have left about 350 books, many of which have survived. Among them are works on the pulse, the circulation of the blood, eczema, gout, and **anatomy**.

Galen was born in Pergamum, in what is now Turkey. His family was wealthy, so he was able to visit famous medical teachers in many parts of the Mediterranean. His first job was as **physician** to a team of gladiators.

This stone carving shows a midwife helping a woman to give birth. The midwife would clean the newborn baby with olive oil, examine it to make sure it was healthy, and wrap it in a cloth.

The influence of Galen

"It is I, and I alone, who have revealed the true path of medicine," wrote Galen. His texts contain many new theories about how the body worked. For example, he discovered that the **arteries** contain blood as well as the veins. He also stated that a "double-hammer" pulse showed a weakness in the heart (which doctors now call arrhythmia).

Galen's ideas about anatomy and the treatment of disease formed the basis of medical practice until the Middle Ages and beyond. However, many of his ideas were later proved to be wrong. His belief that blood was made in the **liver** was a mistake. He defended the old theory that the body was ruled by four humors. Finally, he thought that **bloodletting** (the cutting of veins to release blood) was the best way to treat many diseases. In fact, it left the patient weaker.

FEMALE DOCTORS

Throughout the Roman Empire, women as well as men worked as doctors. There are tomb inscriptions describing women as *medica* (Latin for "female healer"). They were perhaps only allowed to treat other women, children, and slaves, or they concentrated on female problems, such as diseases of the breast. Female **midwives** helped mothers in childbirth.

WORD STATION
liver large gland in the body that does many important things, such as breaking down sugars and filtering the blood

37

Roman surgery

Surgeons in Rome were clearly skilled in many kinds of operations. Various writings by doctors describe how to amputate (cut off) damaged limbs and how to repair hernias (**organs** poking through the stomach wall). There are accounts of operating on the skull, and even of delicate eye **surgery**.

The biggest source of detail about Roman surgery is a book by a doctor named Celsus, who was writing in about 30 CE. It covers all of medicine but includes descriptions of operations (such as removing bladder stones and tonsils). A section on dentistry also explains how to wire loose teeth into place.

Roman surgeons developed as many as 200 different tools for use in surgery and other operations. There was a wide variety of knives, **scalpels**, and saws, each with a special purpose. Probes allowed the doctor to look inside mouths and other openings. Some tools were very complex, such as a clamp for slowly resetting dislocated joints.

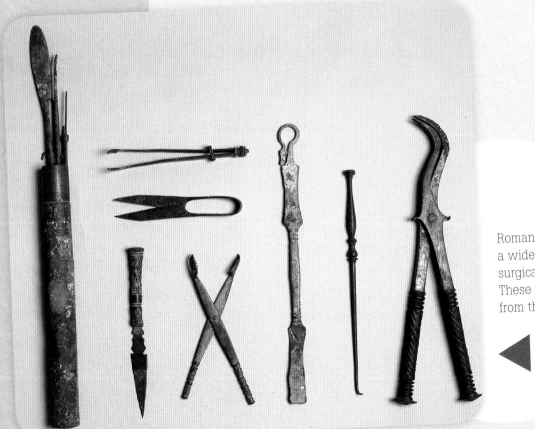

Roman doctors used a wide variety of surgical instruments. These examples date from the 100s CE.

WORD STATION
scalpel sharp cutting tool used by surgeons

In this stone carving, a physician is examining a patient with an eye injury. Roman doctors could treat many kinds of eye problems, including cataracts, ingrown eyelashes, and infections.

▶

Herbal cures and drugs

Doctors used drugs to treat disease and injuries. Many of these were made from common ingredients, such as honey, eggs, cow dung, and a wide variety of herbs. Others needed more exotic and expensive materials. They were often brought from distant parts of the Roman Empire, such as **myrrh** from Egypt and wolfberry from India.

These are mentioned in Roman herbals (catalogs of plants that can be used in medicine). The biggest of these was written by Dioscorides in about 64 CE. He lists over 1,000 substances that can be used as drugs, including not only plants but also animal products and **minerals**. Dioscorides mentions the use of wine and **opium** as painkillers.

TREATING MENTAL PATIENTS

Insanity was familiar to the Romans, both in myths and stories and in everyday life. Those with mental problems were either cared for at home or left to wander the streets. Treatment varied enormously. Some doctors blamed madness on an imbalance of the humors and advised bloodletting and drugs. Some tried calmer methods, such as massage, special diets, and soothing thoughts from philosophy. A few believed the insane should be shocked out of their madness with brutal treatments such as starving, stoning, or beating.

WORD STATION
opium drug made from poppies that has a strong effect on the brain and was used by doctors to relieve pain

39

Fresh water and drains

The Romans knew the importance of public health. For example, between 312 BCE and 226 CE, 11 huge **aqueducts** were built to bring fresh water to the center of Rome. There were also public toilets and a sewage system to carry away waste.

Many towns also had public baths. Regular bathing was seen as a normal part of people's lives, and most went to the bathhouse every day. Doctors encouraged patients to keep clean and fit, to eat plain food, and to avoid rich and spicy dishes. In addition to hot and cold baths and steam rooms, there were gyms and other exercise areas.

The ancient world and after

Medicine had come a long way. The earliest hunter-gatherers probably suffered much less from disease than we do. **Epidemics** of infection only took hold when people had begun to live together in large communities and to travel widely. Bacteria and other infections could pass more easily from person to person.

At first, people had blamed sickness on the gods and other supernatural forces. Gradually, doctors had come to realize that the causes of disease were natural and could be treated naturally. This rational approach to medicine inspired many advances in the civilizations of ancient Greece and Rome.

The Romans built public baths in many cities throughout their huge empire. These ruins are in modern-day Libya.

WORD STATION
aqueduct bridge or channel for moving water from one place to another

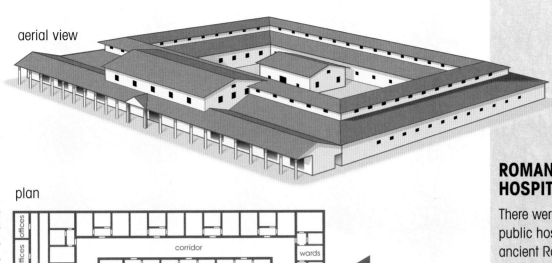

aerial view

plan

offices
offices
offices
offices
entrance
offices
offices
offices

corridor

wards

wards

courtyard

treatment
room

wards

wards

corridor

0   5   10 meters
0   10   20   30 feet

This is the plan of a Roman military hospital, based on excavations of a fortress in Switzerland. Archaeologists do not know for certain what all the rooms were used for, but the pattern of wards holding several patients is found at several sites.

ROMAN HOSPITALS

There were no public hospitals in ancient Rome. Large households often had their own sick rooms, called *valetudinaria*, for slaves. The Roman army provided the first true hospitals, but these were only for sick or wounded soldiers (see the illustration at left). Wealthy people could pay to be treated in a doctor's house. Most poor Romans could not afford health care.

The Roman Empire in the West was destroyed by Germanic invaders in about 476 CE. After this, many of the writings of ancient physicians were lost or forgotten. Their public health systems of bathing and clean water supplies were also largely destroyed. Even so, doctors continued to use the methods that had been passed down by Hippocrates and Galen for many centuries. However, the main advances in medicine were to come from a new civilization — the Islamic world of the Middle East.

Timeline

BCE	
c. 2 million	Small groups of human hunter-gatherers roam the landscape
c. 8000	People begin to develop the earliest human settlements and farming techniques. This encourages the spread of disease.
c. 3500	The earliest civilizations begin in Mesopotamia
c. 3000	Egypt is unified under one king for the first time
c. 2700	Imhotep, builder of the Step Pyramid at Saqqara, develops medical treatments
c. 1780	The Babylonian King Hammurabi orders his Code of Laws to be carved on a pillar
c. 1600	The Edwin Smith papyrus, detailing Egyptian medical practices, is written
c. 1550	The Ebers papyrus is written
c. 1020	The Hebrew civilization is founded in present-day Israel
c. 800	The ancient Greek civilization is established
776	The first Olympic Games take place in Greece
c. 750	Homer's epic *The Iliad* is written
c. 660	Assyrian King Assurbanipal establishes a library of clay tablets, which includes many about medical treatments
c. 500	The Aryan civilization controls much of North India The cult of Asklepios becomes popular in Greece
c. 470	Alcmaeon of Sicily states that the brain is the chief **organ** of feeling in the body

c. 460	The Greek Democritus suggests the theory of atoms Hippocrates is born on the island of Kos
c. 450	Empedocles of Sicily describes the four **humors** of the human body
430–426	The Great Plagues of Athens occur
331	Alexander the Great founds the city of Alexandria in Egypt
c. 300	Herophilus and Erasistratus **dissect** human corpses and advance knowledge of **anatomy**
221	China is united for the first time under a single emperor
c. 200	The text of *The Yellow Emperor's Book* is written
c. 100	The texts of the *Caraka Samhita* and *Susruta Samhita* are written Rome completes the conquest of much of the Mediterranean, including Greece The Greek **physician** Asclepiades arrives in Rome
CE	
c. 30	The Roman Celsus writes an eight-volume encyclopedia, *On Medicine*
c. 64	The Greek Dioscorides publishes a five-volume study of drugs, *Medical Materials*
129	Galen is born in Pergamum, in present-day Turkey
162	Galen arrives in Rome
216	Galen dies
476	End of the Roman Empire in the West

Glossary

acupuncture Chinese treatment in which fine needles are inserted at special points on the body

anatomy bodily structure of a human, animal, or plant

aqueduct bridge or channel for moving water from one place to another

artery blood vessel that carries blood away from the heart

bile bitter liquid produced by the liver, which helps the digestion of food

bloodletting cutting veins to release blood

diagnose identify the nature of a disease or injury through examination

dislocate move a bone from its normal position

dissect cut up a dead body in order to examine it

duodenum part of the small intestine that plays an important part in digesting food

embalmer someone who preserves a dead body by removing the internal organs and drying out the flesh with chemicals

embryo animal in the very early stages of its development from a fertilized egg

endoscope narrow instrument for examining the inside of the body

epidemic rapid spread of a disease through an area or population

epilepsy disorder of the brain that can cause sudden attacks of convulsive movement

Hippocratic Oath oath taken by a doctor, promising to observe a code of medical behavior based on the teachings of Hippocrates

humor (in ancient medicine) one of the four important fluids that control the body

hygiene practice of maintaining health and preventing disease by keeping clean

kidney stone hard object made of crystallized salts that forms in the kidney

liver large gland in the body that does many important things, such as breaking down sugars and filtering the blood

microbe tiny organism (living thing) that can carry disease

midwife specially trained nurse who assists women in childbirth

mineral natural inorganic (non-living) substance, such as coal

myrrh perfumed substance from trees found in the Middle East and Egypt

nutrient substance that feeds or nourishes something

opium drug made from poppies that has a strong effect on the brain and was used by doctors to relieve pain

organ (of the body) one of the parts of the body that has a special function, such as the heart

physician person qualified to practice medicine

prostate gland in male animals that helps with reproduction

psychiatry study of diseases of the mind

scalpel sharp cutting tool used by surgeons

shaman medicine man or priest who is believed to communicate with the spirit world

smallpox infectious disease that causes blisters on the face and often leads to death

sorcery taking action by communicating with the world of spirits, as in witchcraft

surgery treatment of an injury or disease by a manual operation rather than drugs

symptom feeling or other sign that shows that a person has a disease

Find Out More

Books

Catel, Patrick. *What Did the Ancient Greeks Do For Me?* (Linking the Past and Present). Chicago: Heinemann Library, 2011.

Catel, Patrick. *What Did the Ancient Romans Do For Me?* (Linking the Past and Present). Chicago: Heinemann Library, 2011.

Elliott, James. *Outlines of Greek and Roman Medicine.* Charleston, S.C.: BiblioBazaar, 2007.

Hartman, Eve, and Wendy Meshbesher. *The Scientists Behind Medical Advances* (Sci-Hi Scientists). Chicago: Raintree, 2011.

Kelly, Kate. *Early Civilizations: Prehistoric Times to 500 CE* (History of Medicine). New York: Facts on File, 2010.

Web sites

www.historyforkids.org/learn/china/science/chinamedicine.htm
Learn more about medicine in ancient China at this web site.

www.historyforkids.org/learn/india/science/medicine.htm
This web site contains lots of information about medical practices in ancient India.

www.knowitall.org/kidswork/hospital/history/ancient/index.html
This web site contains a brief guide to ancient medicine.

www.yourdiscovery.com/greece/science_and_medicine/index.shtml
This web site is full of facts about ancient Greek medicine.

Places to visit

The Exploratorium, San Francisco, California
www.exploratorium.edu

The Health Museum, Houston, Texas
www.mhms.org

International Museum of Surgical Science, Chicago, Illinois
www.imss.org

Metropolitan Museum of Art, New York City
www.metmuseum.org

National Museum of Health and Medicine, Washington, D.C.
nmhm.washingtondc.museum

More topics to research

- What does a shaman actually do?

- What evidence is left that tells us about Romans baths and aqueducts?

- How widely is traditional Chinese medicine still used in modern China?

- What really happened in the Great Plague of Athens?

- The cover of this book shows a detail of a fresco from the ancient Roman city of Pompeii. The fresco depicts the hero Aeneas wounded in battle, as described in the epic poem the *Aeneid*. Find out more about the figures in the painting and the story behind the scene. You could also research the kinds of instruments ancient Roman doctors used on battlefields.

Index